ROCKY MO
NATIONAL PARK
TRAVEL GUIDE
2023

DISCOVER THE MAJESTIC
BEAUTY OF ROCKY
MOUNTAIN NATIONAL PARK:
YOUR ULTIMATE TRAVEL
GUIDE 2023

ERIC B. HERNANDEZ

TABLE OF CONTENTS

Chapter 1. Introduction..................................**5**

Planning Your Trip....................................... 7

Chapter 2. Understanding Rocky Mountain National Park...**10**

Park Overview....................................... 10

Geology and Natural History....................12

Climate and Weather............................... 14

Chapter 3. Getting There...........................**19**

Transportation Options............................ 19

Driving to the Park............................... 19

Flying to Nearby Airports...................... 21

Public Transportation...........................22

Maps and Trails.. 23

Chapter 4. Best Time to Visit.....................**28**

Seasonal Highlights....................................28

Summer Adventures............................28

Fall Foliage and Wildlife Viewing..........30

Winter Activities.................................. 31

Spring Awakening................................32

Crowd Levels and Avoiding Tourist Traps..34

Chapter 5. Accommodations.......................**39**

Lodges and Resorts.................................39

Campgrounds and Backcountry Camping.41

Cabin Rentals and Vacation Homes..........42

Chapter 6. Outdoor Activities......................45

Hiking Trails for All Skill Levels.................45

    Must-Try Day Hikes............................. 46

    Challenging Summit Trails....................47

Wildlife Watching and Photography...........49

Fishing in Rocky Mountain Streams and Lakes.. 51

Rock Climbing and Bouldering.................. 52

Mountain Biking Trails............................. 54

Backpacking Adventures........................... 55

Chapter 7. Adventure and Thrills................57

White Water Rafting.................................57

Horseback Riding Tours............................58

Zip Lining and Aerial Adventure Parks...... 59

Off-Roading and ATV Trails....................... 60

Snowmobiling in Winter............................ 60

Chapter 8. Exploring Nearby Attractions... 62

Estes Park: Gateway to the Rockies......... 62

Grand Lake and Shadow Mountain Lake.. 64

Hot Springs and Wellness Retreats...........65

Historic Sites and Museums...................... 66

Chapter 9. Safety and Wildlife Etiquette.....69

Park Rules and Regulations..................... 70

Safety Precautions in the Wilderness........71

Bear and Wildlife Awareness......................72

Chapter 10. Food and Dining........................75

Best Restaurants and Cafes......................75

Local Cuisine and Food Trucks................ 77

Picnic Spots and BBQ Areas.....................78

Chapter 11. Souvenirs and Shopping......... 80

Gift Shops and Visitor Centers.................. 80

Local Artisans and Crafts..........................82

Chapter 12. Traveling on a Budget..............85

Free and Affordable Activities....................85

Camping and Dining Tips.......................... 87

Chapter 13. Conclusion...............................90

Fond Farewell to Rocky Mountain
National Park... 90

Your Next Adventure............................91

Appendix... 93

Useful Contacts and Emergency Information
....93

Chapter 1. Introduction

Thank you for visiting Rocky Mountain National Park!

Welcome to Rocky Mountain National Park

Rocky Mountain National Park (RMNP), which is located in the heart of the magnificent Rocky Mountains, is a beautiful wilderness destination that appeals to outdoor enthusiasts, intrepid travelers, and nature lovers alike. This national park, which covers over 415 square miles in northern Colorado, is renowned for its varied ecosystems, breathtaking mountain scenery, pure alpine lakes, and an abundance of species.

You'll be welcomed as you enter this pristine paradise by craggy peaks, gushing waterfalls, lush woods, and meadows bursting with colorful wildflowers. RMNP is a paradise for all types of tourists, especially males looking for exhilarating experiences in the great outdoors, thanks to the variety of recreational activities it offers all year long.

About This Guide

This thorough travel manual was created especially for males who want to visit Rocky Mountain National Park in 2023. This guide is your ultimate companion to unlock the finest of RMNP, whether you're an adrenaline addict looking for strenuous hikes, a beginner photographer looking for breathtaking vistas, or a nature lover ready to observe the beauties of the environment.

The best times to visit the park based on seasonal highlights and crowd levels, suggested accommodations to suit your preferences, and a variety of outdoor activities catered to your sense of adventure can all be found in this guide, which provides detailed information on various aspects of your trip.

We'll also explore the neighborhood attractions, which provide the ideal fusion of regional culture, history, and leisure for tourists wishing to continue their exploration outside the national park's boundaries.

Planning Your Trip

Careful planning is the first step to a successful and memorable vacation to RMNP. Here are some crucial actions to take into account:

Identify Your Interests: Choose the kind of park experience you want to have. Are you interested in going on hikes, taking pictures of wildlife, fishing, rock climbing, or just taking in the tranquil beauty of nature?

The Right Time: Rocky Mountain National Park is beautiful all year round. Landscapes are more lush in the summer, while a rainbow of colors can be seen in the fall. Spring delivers blooming wildflowers, while winter brings snow-covered peaks and distinctive winter sports. Pick a time that fits your preferences and areas of interest.

To get there, look into your alternatives for getting around. Plan your itinerary and make sure your car is in good shape if you want to drive. As an alternative, you could fly into adjacent airports and then either hire a car or take a bus.

Lodges, campgrounds, cabins, and vacation houses are just a few of the lodging options available in RMNP. Make arrangements much in advance, especially during busy times, depending on your preferred degree of luxury and distance from nature.

Outdoor Activities: If you love the outdoors, there are a ton of outdoor activities available to you. Make a list of the activities you want to engage in, from leisurely strolls along gorgeous trails to strenuous mountain ascents, and make sure you have the required equipment.

Safety Advice: The park's environment can be unpredictable in addition to its appealing beauty. To guarantee your safety and the preservation of this natural beauty, become familiar with safety precautions, wildlife awareness, and Leave No Trace principles.

Planning your trip within your budget is important. With careful planning, you can have a rewarding time without breaking the bank because of the free and inexpensive activities offered by RMNP.

Let this guide be your go-to resource as you set out on your adventure in Rocky Mountain National Park, enabling you to maximize your trip into the heart of the Rockies. So put on your hiking boots, grab your camera, and prepare to make lifelong memories in this beautiful paradise. Happy adventuring!

Chapter 2. Understanding Rocky Mountain National Park

Park Overview

The crowning achievement of the American national park system is Rocky Mountain National Park (RMNP). RMNP, which was founded on January 26, 1915, covers a portion of Colorado's Larimer, Grand, and Boulder counties. The park, which spans an area of over 415 square miles, offers an astounding diversity of topography, ecosystems, and species.

The renowned Rocky Mountains, which dominate the skyline with spectacular peaks soaring beyond 14,000 feet, are the park's defining feature. Geologic processes that occurred over millions of years have resulted in these towering mountains, which provide visitors with a spectacular backdrop.

RMNP 2023

The Continental Divide, a tall ridge dividing the watersheds running into the Pacific Ocean from those flowing into the Atlantic Ocean, cuts across RMNP. A more arid environment and lower elevation are features of the park's eastern edge, often known as the Front Range. The scenery is lush and dotted with several alpine lakes and flowing waterfalls on the western side, sometimes referred to as the West Slope.

There are numerous natural beauties within the park's limits, including over 150 mountain peaks, 77 of which are higher than 12,000 feet. Longs Peak, the park's tallest peak at an astounding 14,259 feet, is a haven for seasoned mountaineers.

RMNP is recognized for its various ecosystems, which change greatly with elevation and are in addition to its breathtaking mountain landscape. The park is a hotspot for biodiversity because it contains a variety of ecosystems, from delicate alpine tundra through subalpine forests of spruce and fir to spruce and fir subalpine forests.

Geology and Natural History

Rocky Mountain National Park's geology offers an enthralling window into the Earth's turbulent past. The rocks in the park are over a billion years old, and the current environment is the product of geological processes that took place over a long period of time.

The Precambrian rocks that make up the park's foundation are some of the oldest on the continent and were created by ancient oceans, volcanic activity, and extremely high pressure and heat. These old rocks were gradually exposed by uplift and erosion, resulting in the breathtaking cliffs and rough terrain found in locations like the Lumpy Ridge region.

Rocks were folded and faulted to form the magnificent peaks and valleys that are still visible today as a result of the ascent of the Rocky Mountains some 70 million years ago. The park's environment was significantly affected by glaciers throughout the Ice Ages, who carved out vast valleys and left behind U-shaped canyons, cirques, and moraines.

The many ecosystems present in the park at various elevations are influenced by the unique geology of the area. You will come across different flora and wildlife that are adapted to their individual settings as you climb from the montane forests to the subalpine and alpine regions.

The natural history of Rocky Mountain National Park is similarly fascinating. Several Native American cultures used the park's resources for hunting and gathering thousands of years ago, according to archeological evidence. The discovery of this natural beauty dates back to the mid-1800s, when European exploration and settlement started.

In order to preserve this pristine wilderness for future generations, conservation efforts in the late 19th and early 20th centuries resulted in the creation of Rocky Mountain National Park. The park still serves as a symbol of the value of protecting natural areas for exploration and pleasure as well as for scientific research.

Consider the eternal beauty and intricacy of the Earth's processes as you learn about the geology and natural history of Rocky Mountain National Park. These processes have produced this breathtaking environment. Every step you take is a trip through the ages, linking you with the history and present of this unique national park, whether you're hiking among ancient rocks or admiring the majestic mountains.

Climate and Weather

The Rocky Mountain National Park's (RMNP) high elevation and rugged topography have an impact on the climate and weather there. Visitors should be ready for a broad range of conditions, even within a single day, because the park's weather can be quite varied and can change quickly.

Temperature and Elevation

The park has an elevation range of over 14,000 feet (4,267 meters) in the highest peaks to about 7,500 feet (2,286 meters) in the mountain regions. Generally speaking, the temperatures drop as you go higher. Every 1,000 feet of elevation rise results in a 3 to 5 degree Fahrenheit temperature drop on average. This means that higher elevations can experience relatively chilly temperatures throughout the year, especially at night.

Seasons

Four distinct seasons are experienced in Rocky Mountain National Park:

Spring (March to May): With the melting of the snow and the blooming of the wildflowers, spring is a period of awakening in the park. However, early in the season, snowfall may still occur at higher elevations.

Summer (June to August): The park's meadows are bursting with wildflowers at this time, and hiking routes are open to all visitors. Daytime temperatures can range from pleasant to warm at lower elevations, but they can still be cool at higher elevations. In the summer, afternoon thunderstorms are frequent.

Fall (September to November): Aspen trees in the park change to vivid shades of golden and gold in the fall, creating a spectacle of color. Even while the days are frequently sunny and pleasant, it gets very cold, especially at higher altitudes and in the evenings.

Winter in RMNP is a white wonderland (December to February). As a result of the park's frequent snowfall, fans of winter sports flock there. However, due to snow and road restrictions, some park sites, especially those at higher elevations, might not be accessible.

Precipitation

The majority of the park's precipitation falls as snow throughout the winter months. However, during the spring and summer, it can also encounter rain and thunderstorms. Summer afternoon thunderstorms are frequent and can bring abrupt changes in the weather, such as lightning, hail, and heavy rain.

Wind

Strong and gusty winds are common in Rocky Mountain National Park, especially at higher altitudes. Visitors need to be prepared for windy situations because wind speeds can considerably rise on exposed mountain slopes and peaks.

Climate Readiness

- Visitors are encouraged to be well-prepared for their visits because the weather in the Rocky Mountains is erratic. Here are a few advices:

- To adapt to the varying temperatures throughout the day, dress in layers.

- Even on sunny days, have rain gear and a waterproof jacket handy.

- Before leaving, always check the weather forecast to be informed of any potential weather advisories or warnings.

- Bring lots of water, food, and additional clothing to stay warm and dry whether climbing or traveling to higher altitudes.

- Observe the park's rules and weather-related advisories, particularly during thunderstorms and winter storms.

A safe and pleasurable visit to Rocky Mountain National Park depends on having a good understanding of its environment and weather. Being ready for the shifting weather will guarantee that you get the most out of your experience in this breathtaking and dynamic wilderness, whether you're traveling during the hot summer months or brave the winter wonderland.

Chapter 3. Getting There

Transportation Options

Rocky Mountain National Park offers a variety of transportation options.

How to get to Rocky Mountain National Park is one of the key factors to take into account while making travel plans. Travel choices may be impacted by the park's isolated location and enormous size. The following are the main ways to get to RMNP through transportation:

Driving to the Park

Driving to Rocky Mountain National Park is a well-liked choice since it offers ease and flexibility, especially for visitors who want to take their time and explore the park. When traveling by car to RMNP, keep the following in mind:

Access Points: The park has a number of entrances, the most well-known of which are the Grand Lake Entrance on the west side and the Beaver Meadows Entrance on the east side, close to Estes Park. Fall River, Wild Basin, and the Colorado River Trailhead are other entrances.

Estes Park: The town of Estes Park acts as the entrance to RMNP if you are traveling from the east. It provides a range of lodging choices, dining alternatives, and visitor services.

Grand Lake: The town of Grand Lake offers housing and food options for visitors arriving from the west and allows access to the park's western side.

Scenic Drives: The drive to RMNP is beautiful and scenic, offering opportunities to take in breathtaking views of the local fauna and landscapes. For instance, the Trail Ridge Road, the highest continuous paved road in the United States, connects the east and west sides of the park and provides stunning panoramas.

Road Conditions: Before starting your trip, it's important to verify the status of the roads and any potential closures, especially in the winter when some roads can be closed due to snow.

Parking: It is advised to arrive early in the day to reserve parking spaces because the park's popular areas might grow busy. Additionally, shuttle systems can be in place during busy times to ease traffic and parking difficulties.

Flying to Nearby Airports

Flying to local airports is an alternative for those coming from a distance. the following two airports are the main entry points to Rocky Mountain National Park:

The largest airport in the area is **Denver International Airport (DEN),** which is situated about 70 miles southeast of RMNP. Visitors can rent a car from this location and travel 1.5 to 2 hours to the park, depending on traffic and road conditions.

Eagle County Regional Airport (EGE): Eagle County Regional Airport is located roughly 110 miles west of RMNP and serves the Vail Valley region. Although it provides a more direct approach to the park's western gate, the drive can take up to three hours.

Public Transportation

While most visitors to the park go by private vehicle, there are a few public transportation options available:

RMNP Shuttle Buses: RMNP runs a free shuttle bus service inside the park during the busiest travel times. These shuttles run between several trailheads, visitor centers, and tourist attractions, which helps to ease traffic and parking difficulties. From late May until early October, the shuttle service generally operates.

Estes Park Shuttle: The town of Estes Park runs a shuttle service that provides access to the park's tourist centers and connects other sites inside the town.

Public Transportation from surrounding Towns: If you don't want to drive into the park, you can take public transportation from certain surrounding towns and cities that connect to Estes Park or Grand Lake.

The effort required to get to Rocky Mountain National Park is well worth it, regardless of the mode of transportation you select. When you arrive in this natural wonderland, you'll be rewarded with an unforgettable experience in the heart of the Rockies. The drive there is full of beautiful beauty.

Maps and Trails

The next stage after reaching Rocky Mountain National Park is to efficiently negotiate its vast and varied terrain. It's crucial to know the park's trail network inside and out and to use the tools at your disposal if you want to get the most out of your trip and have a safe and happy time.

Maps

RMNP provides visitors with a number of maps to aid in exploring the park. It is strongly advised to obtain a thorough map from one of the visitor centers or the park's official website before embarking on any trip. Here are a few crucial maps to take into account:

A general map of the park, a list of the park's main attractions, and important details regarding park rules and safety are all included in the park brochure, which is accessible at entrance stations and tourist centers.

Trail Maps: At the tourist centers and trailheads, specific trail maps are offered. These maps detail specific hiking routes, including their lengths, degrees of difficulty, and notable landmarks. When hiking, you must always have a trail map with you because it will help you plan your route and navigate.

Topographic charts provide precise information about the topography, elevation changes, and geographic characteristics of the park for more seasoned hikers and backcountry explorers. You can purchase topographic maps from bookstores, outdoor supply stores, or online resources.

Trails

Over 350 miles of hiking trails, ranging from leisurely strolls to strenuous backcountry excursions, may be found in Rocky Mountain National Park. Every trail presents a different angle on the park's varied topography, wildlife, and natural beauties. When selecting and traveling paths, keep the following important factors in mind:

Trail Difficulty: Based on length, elevation gain, and topography, trails in RMNP are often divided into easy, moderate, and severe categories. To ensure a secure and pleasurable trip, pick a track that is appropriate for your expertise and fitness level.

Route Conditions: In particular at higher elevations, weather and seasonal fluctuations can have an impact on route conditions. For the most recent information on trail closures, trailhead access, and potential dangers, contact the visitor centers.

Safety Advice: Let someone know your plans and anticipated return time before starting any hike. Bring along the necessary safety gear, such as a first aid kit, extra water, snacks, and layers of clothes. Be ready for rapid changes in the weather, especially when afternoon thunderstorms are in the forecast.

Respect Wildlife and Leave No Trace: Keep a safe distance when viewing wildlife, and never approach or feed it. To reduce your environmental impact and protect the park's natural beauty for future generations, adhere to the Leave No Trace guidelines.

Backcountry Permits: You'll need a backcountry permit if you intend to camp in the wilderness or go on multi-day hikes. Permits are necessary for regulating backcountry use and guaranteeing visitor security and can be obtained from the park's wilderness offices.

In addition to its breathtaking scenery, Rocky Mountain National Park is beautiful because it offers the chance to get close to nature and spend time outdoors. You can have life-changing experiences and make the most of your time in this mesmerizing natural wonderland by using the park's maps and trails wisely and following safety precautions.

Chapter 4. Best Time to Visit

Seasonal Highlights

Rocky Mountain National Park is a year-round destination because it provides a distinctive and alluring experience in every season. Every season has its own unique set of highlights, giving visitors a variety of chances to discover the park's natural beauties.

Summer Adventures

In Rocky Mountain National Park, summer is the busiest travel period, and for good reason. The park comes alive with lush vegetation, blooming wildflowers, and a variety of outdoor activities from late June to early September. Here are some summertime activities you may take part in in RMNP:

Summer is the ideal season for hiking in the park because most routes are open and free of snow. There are possibilities for all skill levels, ranging from casual strolls to strenuous peak excursions. The Alpine Ridge Trail, Bear Lake Loop, and Emerald Lake Trail are a few well-liked day walks.

Viewing Animals: The park is a great place to see wildlife during the summer. Elk, mule deer, bighorn sheep, and various bird species are to be on the lookout for. The greatest times to see wildlife are in the early morning and late at night.

Wildflower Displays: During the summer, the park's meadows explode with color. The vistas are decorated with wildflowers like columbine, paintbrush, and lupine, making for beautiful photo opportunities.

Trail Ridge Road, a picturesque road that runs through the park, is completely open in the summer. Along the route, there are possibilities to witness wildlife, alpine tundra, and spectacular views of the surrounding mountains.

Fall Foliage and Wildlife Viewing

Rocky Mountain National Park experiences a magnificent season in the fall when the trees transform into a dazzling display of fall colors. The peak of the fall foliage often happens in late September or early October. The following are some of the attractions to see in the fall:

Aspens predominate in the park's woodlands, which turn a golden-yellow in the fall, making it a photographer's dream. The Cub Lake Trail, the West Elk Loop, and the Bierstadt Lake Trail are a few of the best places to see autumn foliage.

Elk Rut: The male elk's mating season, during which they bugle and fight bloody mating bouts, occurs in the fall. The meadows of Horseshoe Park and Moraine Park are well-liked locations to spot this unusual wildlife behavior.

Quieter Trails: While the park can get packed in the summer, it is less crowded in the fall. You'll get the chance to take advantage of more tranquil pathways and a wilderness experience.

Winter Activities

Rocky Mountain National Park's scenery is transformed into a winter wonderland in the winter, opening up a whole new range of experiences and activities. Snow has forced the closure of some park sections, but there are still many of chances for winter adventures:

Cross-country Skiing and Snowshoeing: During the winter, many trails are used as cross-country skiing and snowshoeing routes. Winter activities are common in the Bear Lake region and at the trailhead for Glacier Gorge.

Tracking wildlife is a great activity when there is snow on the ground since it makes animal footprints more noticeable.

Winter Photography: The park's snow-covered vistas, frozen lakes, and frost-covered trees provide photographers with exceptional chances to capture breathtaking winter pictures.

Spring Awakening

Rocky Mountain National Park experiences rejuvenation and reawakening in the spring. The park comes alive with new vegetation and wildlife activity as the winter melts and the weather rises. Here are a few reasons to travel during the springtime:

Waterfalls: The park's waterfalls experience enhanced water flow in the spring, which makes it the perfect time to admire their beauty and power. The two most well-known places to observe spring waterfalls are Alberta Falls and Ouzel Falls.

Wildlife Sightings: Spring is an active and noticeable season for a variety of creatures. Watch for young animals including elk calves and lambs of bighorn sheep, as well as migratory bird species coming back to the park.

Wildflowers: The park's wildflowers begin to bloom when the snow melts, decorating the meadows with vivid hues. Spring wildflower displays can be found in abundance along the Cub Lake Trail and in the Wild Basin region.

Spring Hiking: Lower elevation walks are doable in the spring, even if some higher mountain paths may still be covered in snow. It's a wonderful time to hike trails like the Lily Lake Loop and the Gem Lake Trail.

The best time to visit Rocky Mountain National Park depends on your interests and preferences because each season has its own distinct appeal. RMNP offers something remarkable to offer all year long, whether you're looking for colorful wildflowers, breathtaking fall colors, or winter wonderlands. You'll be rewarded with unforgettable experiences in this majestic wilderness if you plan your vacation wisely.

Crowd Levels and Avoiding Tourist Traps

In Rocky Mountain National Park, how crowded it is and how to avoid tourist traps

With millions of tourists each year, Rocky Mountain National Park is a well-liked location thanks to its stunning natural surroundings and varied landscapes. Even though the park is well-deservedly popular, there is a chance that some places will get congested, especially during the busiest travel times. The following advice can help you manage crowd sizes and stay away from tourist traps:

Selecting the Appropriate Time to Visit

Crowd levels in Rocky Mountain National Park can be significantly influenced by the time of your visit.

The busiest time of year and peak tourist season is from June through August. If at all feasible, try to go in the shoulder seasons of spring (April to May) or fall (September to October), when it's still nice outside and there aren't as many people around. Although there are fewer tourists during the winter months of November to March, some parts of the park could be impassable owing to snow.

Getting There Early or Late

Plan to arrive at popular locations and trailheads early in the morning or later in the afternoon to avoid the busiest times. Since most guests come in the middle of the morning, getting there early can make for a more relaxing and delightful experience.

Investigating Less Visited Areas

There are many less-visited regions of the park that provide equally spectacular scenery and possibilities for seclusion, despite the fact that some spots, such as Bear Lake and Trail Ridge Road, are extremely popular. To avoid the crowds, think about exploring undiscovered areas and off-the-beaten-path hikes.

Making Use of Shuttle Services

Rocky Mountain National Park runs shuttle services during the busiest travel times to lessen traffic and parking difficulties. Use the shuttle service to go to well-known locations like Bear Lake and Glacier Gorge and take it easy without having to worry about parking.

Lesser-Known Trails for Hiking

Consider venturing into the park's less-traveled regions rather than sticking to the most popular routes. Although these trails might take more work to reach, they frequently provide a more individualized and fulfilling wilderness experience.

Overnighting in the Park

If at all possible, think about spending the night in the park. Campgrounds, lodges, cottages, and backcountry camping are available as lodging choices. Spending the night will give you the chance to visit the park in the morning and evening when it's less crowded.

Respecting Nature and Wildlife

Respect wildlife and follow Leave No Trace guidelines to prevent adding to crowds. Keep to the trails that have been established, stay away from wildlife, and pack out all rubbish. By being aware of your environmental impact, you help to create a more enjoyable and sustainable experience for everyone.

Make a Plan and be Adaptable

Plan your trip in advance, taking into account possible substitute locations and activities. Be flexible with your schedule, though. Your plans might need to be modified as a result of the weather, road closures, and other circumstances. Be open to explore new opportunities in the park and embrace serendipity.

RMNP 2023

You may fully experience the natural splendor and tranquility of Rocky Mountain National Park by being proactive and cautious about regulating crowd levels and avoiding tourist traps. Discover why this wonderful park is still a beloved destination for adventurers and nature lovers from all over the world by embracing the peace of the woods.

Chapter 5. Accommodations

Rocky Mountain National Park Lodgings

Rocky Mountain National Park provides a range of lodging options to accommodate various tastes and price ranges. There are choices available to improve your time in the park, whether you like the conveniences of a warm lodge, the rustic charm of camping, or the privacy of a vacation home.

Lodges and Resorts

Visitors have the easy and comfortable option of staying in one of the lodges or resorts located inside or close to the park. These lodging options frequently provide quick access to well-liked sites as well as breathtaking panoramas of the surroundings. The following are some significant inns and resorts in Rocky Mountain National Park:

The Stanley Hotel is a historic landmark in Estes Park that is known for being the inspiration for Stephen King's novel "The Shining." The Stanley Hotel features opulent accommodations, superb dining, and stunning views of the surrounding mountains.

YMCA of the Rockies: Located on the east side of the park, close to the Fall River Entrance, the YMCA of the Rockies offers a family-friendly and reasonably priced hotel choice. They provide lodging options for visitors in the form of lodge rooms, holiday houses, and cabins.

The Estes Park Resort is a lakefront resort with a variety of amenities, including a restaurant, spa, and outdoor pool. It is nestled on the banks of Lake Estes.

Grand Lake Lodge: Grand Lake Lodge offers a rustic mountain experience with cabin rooms and breathtaking views of the lake and mountains. It is located on the west side of the park, overlooking Grand Lake.

Campgrounds and Backcountry Camping

Camping is a well-liked activity in Rocky Mountain National Park for people looking for a more unique and adventurous experience. A range of campgrounds are available in the park, from conventional campgrounds with facilities to backcountry camping for a more secluded experience. Here are some choices for camping:

Built-in Campgrounds: The RMNP has a number of built-in campgrounds, each with its own special characteristics. Campgrounds like Moraine Park Campground, Glacier Basin Campground, and Aspenglen Campground are a few of the well-liked ones. Usually, these campgrounds have amenities like fire rings, picnic tables, and restrooms.

Backcountry Camping: Backcountry camping is a great option for seasoned campers seeking a more private experience. Backcountry camping calls for permits, which are available from the park's wilderness offices. It's crucial to abide by all rules for wilderness camping and the Leave No Trace philosophy.

Cabin Rentals and Vacation Homes

In the adjacent towns and communities surrounding the park, cabin rentals and vacation houses are accessible to those looking for additional privacy and a home-away-from-home experience. Cozy cottages and expansive vacation homes with mountain views are both available in Estes Park and Grand Lake.

For further convenience and more room for families or groups, consider renting a cabin or vacation home. These accommodations frequently have features like hot tubs, fireplaces, and outside lounging spaces.

Reservation Tips

Due to Rocky Mountain National Park's popularity, bookings should be made well in advance, especially during the busiest travel times. Here are some suggestions for reservations:

Reservations for Lodges and Resorts: If you intend to stay in a lodge or resort inside the park, book as far in advance as you can, sometimes up to a year, to guarantee your preferred dates and lodging.

Reservations for campgrounds are recommended because they can get busy, particularly in the summer. By using the National Recreation Reservation System (NRRS) or the park's official website, you can reserve a campsite.

Wilderness Camping Permits: If you intend to camp in the wilderness, get your permit as soon as possible because there is a strong demand and limited supply, particularly for popular camping areas.

Booking a cabin or vacation house in a nearby town necessitates ahead planning, particularly during busy times of year.

You'll have the chance to select the right lodging for your vacation in Rocky Mountain National Park if you plan ahead and book early. The range of lodging options in and around the park guarantees that you'll find the ideal place to make your stay memorable and enjoyable, whether you're looking for luxury, adventure, or a quiet mountain getaway.

Chapter 6. Outdoor Activities

Hiking Trails for All Skill Levels

The vast network of hiking trails in Rocky Mountain National Park, which are accessible to hikers of all abilities, is one of the park's main draws. The park has plenty to offer everyone, whether you're a novice searching for a leisurely stroll or an experienced hiker looking for a strenuous adventure.

When trekking in the park, it's necessary to keep in mind the following things:

Altitude: Even short climbs can be more difficult than expected due to the park's high elevation. Take your time, drink plenty of water, and watch out for any symptoms of altitude sickness.

Weather: Be ready for rapid shifts as the weather in the highlands can be erratic. Even in the summer, always check the weather prediction before leaving and pack a few extra layers of clothing.

Wildlife: Several wildlife species can be found in Rocky Mountain National Park. Never approach an animal up close and never give them food. In regions where bears are reputed to be active, carry bear spray.

Must-Try Day Hikes

There are a number of must-try day hikes in Rocky Mountain National Park that offer breathtaking views and unforgettable experiences for tourists wishing to explore the majesty of the park on a shorter trip. Here are a few well-liked day hikes:

Bear Lake Circular: A quick and simple circular hike with stunning views of Hallett Peak and the neighboring peaks. Families and anyone who likes to take a leisurely stroll can consider this as a fantastic choice.

Emerald Lake Trail: This easy trip leads to Nymph Lake, Dream Lake, and Emerald Lake, three stunning alpine lakes. The hike offers breathtaking Rockies vistas, and the early morning light makes it more spectacular.

The Alberta Falls are a beautiful waterfall that cascades over sizable boulders and are accessible via this hike. All levels of hikers can easily access the short trail because of its accessibility.

A simple, wheelchair-accessible trail that circles Sprague Lake offers spectacular reflections of the surrounding mountains as well as the opportunity to see ducks and other wildlife. This trail is called the Sprague Lake Loop.

Challenging Summit Trails

Rocky Mountain National Park offers a number of strenuous summit trails for experienced hikers and mountaineers looking for a more difficult trip. These trails call for the right gear, physical fitness, and understanding of mountain safety. The following are some noteworthy difficult peak trails:

Longs Peak: At 14,259 feet (4,346 meters), Longs Peak is the tallest peak in Rocky Mountain National Park and a popular destination for hikers. The most well-known track to the peak is the Keyhole Route, but it necessitates advanced climbing expertise and an early start.

Hallett Peak: The stunning views of Glacier Gorge and the neighboring peaks are provided by this strenuous trail. The trail is best undertaken by seasoned hikers due to some scrambling and exposed areas.

A challenging trek climbs to Flattop Mountain, which provides sweeping views of the Continental Divide and the lowlands below. Hikers can continue from Flattop Mountain to Hallett Peak or Andrews Glacier.

Notchtop Mountain: This less popular choice for those looking for a summit has steep sections and requires a final scramble to reach the top. Compared to other peaks, the top views are more gratifying and less crowded.

No matter which Rocky Mountain National Park hiking trail you pick, each one provides a special chance to immerse yourself in the park's natural beauty and appreciate the grandeur of the Rocky Mountains. To ensure that this amazing environment is preserved for future generations, always be sure to take the necessary precautions, adhere to safety regulations, and leave no trace.

Wildlife Watching and Photography

For both photographers and wildlife aficionados, Rocky Mountain National Park is a paradise. The park's different ecosystems provide a home to a broad range of creatures, making it a great place to observe and photograph wildlife in its natural settings. Here are some vital pointers for observing wildlife and taking pictures of it in Rocky Mountain:

Respect Wildlife: When viewing wildlife, keep your distance and take pictures with binoculars or a zoom lens. Avoid approaching or feeding the animals because doing so can disrupt their normal behavior and put you in danger.

Greatest Times for Wildlife Viewing: Because animals are most active during these hours, early mornings and late afternoons are the greatest times to watch wildlife. Be calm and tranquil; animals can be startled by quick movements or loud noises.

Common Wildlife: Elk, mule deer, bighorn sheep, moose, coyotes, and different bird species can all be found in Rocky Mountain National Park. Watch for these recognizable Rocky Mountain dwellers.

Different elevations in the park support a variety of wildlife species. Wildlife in Different Ecosystems. Bighorn sheep and pikas, for instance, live in higher elevations, but elk and mule deer are more frequently seen in lower elevations.

Photography Advice: When photographing wildlife, keep a safe distance and use a telephoto lens to get up close and personal. To capture the creatures in their native habitats, pay close attention to lighting and composition.

Fishing in Rocky Mountain Streams and Lakes

Anglers can find good fishing chances in Rocky Mountain National Park. The park is a well-liked location for anglers because of its clear lakes and streams, which are home to a variety of fish species. When fishing in a park, keep the following things in mind:

Fishing Regulations: Read up on the park's fishing rules before setting out with your line. Every angler in Colorado over the age of 16 must have a fishing license, and there are laws regarding catch limits and fishing techniques.

Catch and Release: Catch-and-release fishing is encouraged to protect the park's fragile ecosystems.

To reduce stress, handle fish carefully, use barbless hooks, and swiftly return them to the water.

Popular Fishing Spots: The Big Thompson River, Sprague Lake, and Bear Lake are a few of the most well-liked fishing locations in Rocky Mountain National Park. Trout fishing is possible in the park's numerous streams and lakes, including brook, rainbow, and cutthroat trout.

Fly fishing is a well-liked method in the cool, clear mountain waterways of the park. Bring the right equipment and fly patterns that correspond to the natural insects found in the lakes and streams.

Rock Climbing and Bouldering

Rock climbers and boulderers can find exciting chances at Rocky Mountain National Park. Climbers come to the area from all over the world to scale its craggy cliffs and enormous rocks. For bouldering and rock climbing at the park, keep in mind the following:

Regulations & Permits: Technical rock climbing in selected places requires a climbing permit. Some places may be temporarily closed for the protection of animals or for other reasons, so check with the park officials for the most recent rules and closures.

The Rocky Mountain National Park offers climbs for all levels of experience, from easy routes for beginners to difficult and complicated climbs. Make sure the routes you pick are appropriate for your climbing experience and skill level.

Climbing in the high-alpine setting of the park necessitates careful planning and attention to safety. Check the weather, pack the right gear, and be ready for unforeseen weather changes.

Bouldering: The park's sizable boulder fields offer fantastic bouldering possibilities. Chaos Canyon, Emerald Lake, and Upper Chaos are all well-known bouldering locations.

Mountain Biking Trails

The backcountry of Rocky Mountain National Park can be explored and the park's various landscapes can be experienced by mountain riding. It's crucial to remember that only specific roads and paths are suitable for biking. Consider the following important factors when mountain biking in a park:

Bike Rules: Become familiar with the park's bike rules and designated trails. On some highways and multi-use routes, bicycles are permitted, but they are not allowed on hiking trails.

Trail Conditions: Some terrain can be difficult and steep, demanding more physical fitness and mountain riding expertise. Pick trails based on your skill level and expertise.

Road Biking: Road biking gives breath-taking vistas of the surrounding mountains along scenic routes like Trail Ridge Road. However, be ready for arduous ascents and high altitudes.

Backpacking Adventures

Backpacking in Rocky Mountain National Park is a life-changing event for individuals looking for a more intense wilderness encounter. Backpackers have the chance to travel to inaccessible locations, camp out beneath the stars, and see breathtaking sunrises and sunsets. Here are some vital pointers for backcountry hiking in a park:

Wilderness Permits: A permission is required to camp overnight in the wilderness. The wilderness offices of the park are the place to get permits. Because some zones have limited availability, make your travel arrangements in advance and get your permits early.

Leave No Trace: Follow Leave No Trace guidelines to reduce your environmental impact. Use designated campsites, pack out all rubbish, and don't bother the wildlife.

Carry a water filtration device with you because the water sources in the backcountry may not have been treated and could be contaminated.

Black bears can be seen in Rocky Mountain National Park, therefore it's important to store food correctly and abide by bear safety precautions to avoid interactions.

Weather Preparedness: The weather in the wilderness is unpredictable, so be ready for a wide range of temperatures and unexpected storms.

In Rocky Mountain National Park, backpacking offers a singular chance to disconnect from the outer world and fully experience nature. Plan your trip carefully, abide by park rules, and get ready for an unforgettable backpacking adventure amid the breathtaking Rocky Mountain scenery.

Chapter 7. Adventure and Thrills

Rocky Mountain National Park Offers Thrills and Adventure

There are more than simply tranquil treks and serene vistas in Rocky Mountain National Park. The park offers a variety of thrilling outdoor activities for adrenaline junkies, adding another level of adventure to your visit. These exciting RMNP activities are listed below:

White Water Rafting

Adventure seekers can have a thrilling day white water rafting in the nearby rivers around Rocky Mountain National Park. Both the Colorado River and the neighboring Cache La Poudre River offer exhilarating rapids and breathtaking scenery. Rafting experiences are available for paddlers of all ability levels, from family-friendly tours that are beginner-friendly to more difficult rapids for seasoned paddlers.

Professional rafting tour operators offer supervised excursions, guaranteeing your safety and supplying all necessary gear. The snowmelt increases water flow and produces thrilling rapids during the peak rafting season, which normally lasts from May to August.

Horseback Riding Tours

A distinctive and time-honored approach to appreciate the park's beauty is to explore it on horseback. Several guided horseback riding excursions are offered, taking guests over beautiful routes and offering a new viewpoint of the surroundings. For those who like a leisurely pace and wish to cover more ground, horseback riding is the perfect pastime.

The excursions are led by knowledgeable wranglers and well-trained horses, making them appropriate for riders of all experience levels, including beginners. You can join horseback riding excursions to well-known locations like Moraine Park or the Big Thompson River to experience the solitude of nature.

Zip Lining and Aerial Adventure Parks

Think about zipline and aerial adventure parks, which are close to the park's entrances, for a thrilling experience in the air. In the middle of breathtaking mountain scenery, these parks offer exhilarating zip lines, rope courses, and obstacle courses. Families, parties, and individuals looking for an enjoyable and unique outdoor adventure will find it to be the perfect activity.

Aerial adventure parks frequently offer programs that are appropriate for a variety of age groups and skill levels, making them open to everyone. An exciting way to engage with nature and experience an adrenaline rush while doing so is by zip lining through the treetops and overcoming difficult aerial obstacles.

Off-Roading and ATV Trails

A thrilling way to see the rough terrain and stunning views is for off-road enthusiasts to explore the park's surrounding areas on ATVs (all-terrain vehicles) or off-road vehicles. Off-roading is not permitted inside the national park, although there are public lands and national forests close by that have approved off-roading paths.

While having fun on your off-road trip outside of the park, remember to respect the environment, adhere to all rules, and stay on approved paths.

Snowmobiling in Winter

Snowmobiling is an exhilarating sport when the park is covered in snow during winter. In the vicinity of Rocky Mountain National Park and in the nearby national forests, snowmobiling is a well-liked winter sport. Riders can explore this winter wonderland of snow-covered areas.

All skill levels can take advantage of guided snowmobile rides that let you travel through snowy meadows and along picturesque tracks. It's a great opportunity to see the park's beautiful snow-capped peaks, frozen waterfalls, and wildlife footprints in the wintertime.

The above-mentioned activities are those that can be done outside Rocky Mountain National Park because the park itself has rules and regulations for certain activities. To experience these exhilarating excursions responsibly and sustainably, tourists interested in these activities should look for trustworthy outfitters and tour companies operating outside the park's limits.

Chapter 8. Exploring Nearby Attractions

Investigating Local Attractions

A wide variety of surrounding attractions, each offering a special charm and experience, surround Rocky Mountain National Park. Visitors can extend their national park vacation with extra activities and cultural encounters by exploring these nearby locations. These local attractions are worth checking out:

Estes Park: Gateway to the Rockies

Estes Park, a quaint mountain town known as the "Gateway to the Rockies," is situated near the eastern entrance of Rocky Mountain National Park and offers a range of sights and activities for tourists to enjoy:

Downtown Estes Park: Take a stroll through this charming district to see charming shops, art galleries, and delectable restaurants. Don't pass up the chance to sample the renowned saltwater taffy from one of the neighborhood candy stores.

Take a guided tour of the **Stanley Hotel** to discover its fascinating history and spooky legends. This historic monument is renowned for its gorgeous architecture and served as the inspiration for Stephen King's book "The Shining."

Lake Estes: Take in the magnificent views of the lake and the surrounding mountains while taking a leisurely stroll or bike ride along the Lake Estes Trail. Renting a kayak or a paddleboard is another option for those who want to explore the lake.

Take a ride on the aerial tramway at Estes Park for sweeping views of the town and the mountains nearby.

Performance Park: During the summer, Performance Park, an outdoor amphitheater tucked in a lovely natural environment, hosts cultural activities and live music performances.

Grand Lake and Shadow Mountain Lake

The picturesque village of Grand Lake, which is located close to the shores of both Grand Lake and Shadow Mountain Lake, is located on the western side of Rocky Mountain National Park. Here are some sights and things to do in the region:

Grand Lake Boardwalk: Take a stroll along the picturesque shops, eateries, and art galleries that line this historic boardwalk in the heart of Grand Lake.

Water Sports: Boating, kayaking, fishing, and paddleboarding are all possible at Grand Lake and Shadow Mountain Lake. To appreciate the tranquil splendor of these alpine lakes, you can either rent a boat or go on a guided fishing trip.

Adams Falls: Just a short stroll away from Grand Lake lies the picturesque waterfall known as Adam's Falls. Beautiful views of the Colorado River and the surrounding area are available from the trail.

Rocky Mountain Repertory Theatre: Attend a live performance at this theater, which presents a range of theatrical shows all through the summer.

Hot Springs and Wellness Retreats

Relaxing in natural hot springs can be a refreshing experience after days of hiking and adventure. A soothing approach to soak in the therapeutic waters and indulge in spa treatments is at nearby hot springs and health retreats:

Hot Sulphur Springs is a historic resort with natural hot springs pools that range in temperature.

It is situated immediately outside the park's western entrance.

The mineral-rich hot springs pools at the Hot Sulphur Springs Resort & Spa are the perfect place to unwind. The resort also provides massage and spa services.

A few hours' drive from the park at Pagosa Springs is the **Healing Waters Spa,** which offers a variety of spa services as well as access to mineral hot springs pools.

Historic Sites and Museums

There are various historical sites and museums to see for visitors who are interested in the history and cultural heritage of the region:

The Holzwarth Historic Site, which is situated on the park's western edge, provides a window into the lifestyle of the first Rockies homesteaders. Visitors can learn about the history and way of life of the Holzwarth family through guided tours and displays.

Grand Lake's Kauffman House Museum: This museum chronicles the history of Grand Lake and the neighborhood. Investigate the displays and artifacts that depict the history of the town's early years.

The Estes Park Museum is a great place to learn about the past of Estes Park and the neighborhood. The museum has displays on the local fauna, indigenous peoples, early settlers, and the development of the town.

By combining the natural beauty of Rocky Mountain National Park with cultural insights, leisure, and additional activities to suit different interests, exploring the neighborhood attractions around the park delivers a well-rounded experience. The nearby locations offer a wide range of chances for discovery and enjoyment, whether you're interested in historical monuments, outdoor activities, or simply savoring the charm of mountain communities.

Chapter 9. Safety and Wildlife Etiquette

Wildlife Etiquette and Safety in Rocky Mountain National Park

A pristine environment, Rocky Mountain National Park has a variety of ecosystems and a wealth of fauna. It is crucial to abide by park rules and regulations, take safety precautions in the wilderness, and follow bear and wildlife awareness standards in order to make sure that all visitors have a safe and pleasurable time and to maintain the park's natural resources.

Park Rules and Regulations

Keep to Designated paths: Leaving designated paths can cause soil erosion, harm to delicate vegetation, and disturb the habitats of species. To lessen your impact on the environment, stay on well-traveled paths.

Pack Out Trash: The preservation of the park's pure beauty depends on following Leave No Trace guidelines. To maintain the wilderness clean and prevent wildlife from ingesting human food, carry out all rubbish, including food wrappers and waste.

Pets: Pets are permitted in some areas of the park, but they must always be leashed. Make sure to clean up after your pet and keep them away from wildlife to avoid disturbing or approaching it.

Campfires: Only specified fire rings at established campsites are allowed to be used for campfires.

Before visiting, always confirm the local fire regulations, and never leave a campfire unattended.

Fishing laws: If you intend to fish in the park's streams or lakes, get a fishing license and follow the catch-and-release policies outlined in the laws.

Safety Precautions in the Wilderness

Be ready for dramatic temperature decreases, rain, snow, and strong winds as the weather in the mountains can change quickly. Before your travel, check the weather forecast and pack clothing.

Altitude: Those who haven't been acclimatized to the high elevations of the park may get altitude sickness. When trekking, take your time, drink plenty of water, and pay attention to any symptoms like headache, dizziness, and shortness of breath.

Carry a map, compass, or GPS gadget if you're going into the backcountry, especially. Before beginning your hike, become familiar with the trail's pathways and topography.

Water: Bring a lot of water with you because there might not always be reliable water sources near the paths. For untreated water found in the outdoors, use water purification techniques.

Prepare for emergencies by telling someone where you're going and when you expect to be back. Carry the necessities, such as a first aid kit, whistle, torch, and extra food, in case of emergencies.

Bear and Wildlife Awareness

Black bears are only one of the many wildlife species that call Rocky Mountain National Park home. For your protection and the welfare of the animals, you must respect nature and use bear awareness:

Bears and wolves should be kept at least 100 yards (91 meters) away, and other animals should be kept at least 25 yards (23 meters) away. When photographing wildlife, use binoculars or a zoom lens to get a closer look.

Do Not Feed Wildlife: Feeding wild animals is not only against the law, but it also negatively affects their behavior and health. Food from humans can harm wildlife and result in perilous interactions.

Secure Food and Smelly Things: When camping, place all food, garbage, and scented things in designated food storage lockers or bear-proof containers. This lessens the likelihood of disputes and prevents bears from becoming used to human food.

Hiking in Groups: Hike in packs and generate noise to attract the attention of wildlife. This can lessen the likelihood of interactions and help minimize startling animals.

Bear Spray: In regions where bears are active, carry bear spray. Learn how to use it properly and be ready to use it if a bear encounter arises.

You may have a safe and enjoyable trip at Rocky Mountain National Park by following park regulations, taking safety precautions, and showing consideration for wildlife. Additionally, abiding by these rules guarantees that the park's species and scenic splendor are preserved for future generations to enjoy.

Chapter 10. Food and Dining

Rocky Mountain National Park's Food and Dining Options

Rocky Mountain National Park's outdoor exploration can make you pretty hungry. Thankfully, the park provides a range of food alternatives, including picnic areas and casual cafes, allowing guests to enjoy delectable meals amidst the breathtaking mountain environment.

Best Restaurants and Cafes

Rocky Mountain National Park doesn't have any eateries or cafés inside its borders, although the surrounding towns of Estes Park and Grand Lake have a wide variety of restaurants. Here are a few popular eateries and cafes that are worth visiting:

Estes Park

The Dunraven Inn: Known for its Italian fare and sultry atmosphere, the restaurant serves scrumptious meals like pasta, fish, and steaks.

Bird & Jim delivers modern American cuisine in a stylish and rustic atmosphere. It is a farm-to-table restaurant with a focus on locally produced foods.

Notchtop Bakery & Cafe: Notchtop Bakery & Cafe is a well-liked place for breakfast and lunch. It serves freshly baked products, sandwiches, and salads.

Visit **Smokin' Dave's BBQ & Brew** if you're in the mood for barbecue. Delicious smoked meats and traditional sides are served at Smokin' Dave's.

Grand Lake

The Rapids Lodge and Restaurant offers great dining with a varied cuisine that includes seafood, game meats, and vegetarian alternatives while overlooking the Tonahutu River.

A local favorite for barbecue, **Sagebrush BBQ & Grill** offers succulent ribs, brisket, and pulled pig.

Grand Pizza: If you're craving pizza, Grand Pizza has a variety of delectable pies with different toppings.

Local Cuisine and Food Trucks

You can also discover food carts and restaurants offering both regional and international fare in the nearby towns and neighborhoods surrounding the park. To satiate your palate, keep an eye out for these treats:

Local cuisine: Many eateries in the area take pride in using ingredients and flavors that are native to the area in their dishes. Look for menu choices that include fresh food from nearby farms as well as local game meats like elk or bison.

Food trucks: During the busiest tourist seasons, you might come across food trucks serving a range of fast and delectable dishes, including tacos and gourmet sandwiches. For an easy and tasty bite, keep an eye out for these mobile restaurants.

Picnic Spots and BBQ Areas

Rocky Mountain National Park has various lovely picnic places and designated BBQ areas so that tourists can eat in the great outdoors. Several of the park's well-liked picnic spots include:

Moraine Park: This picturesque valley has a number of picnic areas with grills and tables, making it the ideal location to have lunch or a snack while spotting wildlife.

Glacier Basin: This picnic area, which is close to Bear Lake, includes picnic tables so you may enjoy your food while taking in the breathtaking views.

Upper Beaver Meadows: This more sedate picnic location provides a tranquil environment and a chance to relax amidst the park's natural splendor.

To conserve the wildlife and maintain the park's pure environment, don't forget to pack out all of your picnic's rubbish.

The adjacent towns and designated areas in Rocky Mountain National Park offer a variety of food and dining alternatives to suit any palate, whether you're seeking for a fine dining experience, a taste of local cuisine, or a relaxed picnic surrounded by nature. Enjoy the tastes of the Rockies while taking in this renowned national park's breathtaking vistas.

Chapter 11. Souvenirs and Shopping

Rocky Mountain National Park Souvenirs and Shopping

Visitors can save the mementos of their experience and help regional companies and craftspeople by bringing a piece of Rocky Mountain National Park home with them. There are many chances for shopping and selecting the ideal mementos, from gift shops at visitor centers to distinctive local crafts.

Gift Shops and Visitor Centers

The visitor centers at Rocky Mountain National Park are great places to start your souvenir buying. These facilities frequently contain gift stores with a large selection of goods, such as apparel, books, maps, and instructional supplies. The following are some typical trinkets you may purchase at visitor centers:

T-shirts and Clothing: You can find t-shirts, hoodies, and hats with the recognizable logo of Rocky Mountain National Park or with artwork based on the park's fauna and flora.

Find lovely postcards and prints featuring breath-taking images and artwork of the park's natural beauty. These are wonderful mementos or presents for loved ones.

Books and Guides: The visitor centers stock a variety of educational books and guides that can help you learn more about the park's geology, history, wildlife, and hiking trails.

Stickers and Magnets: Tiny and reasonably priced stickers and magnets with park themes are well-liked keepsakes that are simple to collect or exhibit.

Collectible pins and patches that include images of the park's features and fauna are wonderful compliments to caps, backpacks, and outerwear.

Plush Toys: You can find plush toys of the park's animals, like bears, elk, and marmots, for younger visitors or as gifts for kids.

Keep in mind that revenue from visitor center gift shop purchases frequently supports park conservation and educational activities.

Local Artisans and Crafts

Beyond the official gift shops, there are many independent artists and craftspeople living in the nearby communities of Rocky Mountain National Park. It's possible to find one-of-a-kind, handcrafted souvenirs that perfectly encapsulate the spirit of the park by perusing these artisan shops. Local products and crafts include, for instance:

Pottery & Ceramics: Look for lovely pottery with designs that range from wildlife motifs to landscape sceneries, many of which were inspired by the park's natural splendor.

Woodcraft: Local Rockies flora and fauna are sometimes depicted in elaborate woodwork or hand-carved figures made of wood.

Jewelry: Using metals, crystals, and jewels, local craftspeople may design jewelry that is inspired by the park's natural features.

Paintings and Artwork: Beautiful paintings and artwork portraying the natural beauty of the park may be seen at galleries and studios in the local towns.

Handmade Soaps & Skincare Products: Inspired by the untamed landscape of the Rocky Mountains, several local artisans make soaps and skincare items from natural materials.

Native American Items: Authentic Native American crafts and artifacts, which reflect the rich cultural legacy of the area, may be found in various stores.

In addition to ensuring you bring home an original and genuine keepsake, supporting local artists helps the community's economy and the continuation of age-old trades.

Shopping for souvenirs in and around Rocky Mountain National Park offers a diverse and enlightening experience, with everything from official park products in visitor centers to one-of-a-kind crafts from local artisans. With so many alternatives, you can find the ideal souvenir to remember your time spent in this magnificent national park, whether you're searching for a useful memory, a work of art, or a thoughtful gift.

Chapter 12. Traveling on a Budget

Rocky Mountain National Park Budget Travel

Rocky Mountain National Park visits don't have to be expensive. You may enjoy a wonderful and cheap time in this gorgeous environment with some careful planning and wise decisions.

Free and Affordable Activities

Hiking: One of the finest free ways to appreciate the park's splendor is through hiking. You can select a hiking trail based on your tastes and degree of fitness from a large selection that ranges in length and difficulty.

Scenic Drives: Take a scenic drive across the park to take in the breathtaking views from the comfort of your vehicle. Incredible vistas of the Rocky Mountains may be found along Trail Ridge Road and the Peak-to-Peak Scenic Byway.

Species Watching is completely free. The park is home to a wide variety of species. You can see elk, mule deer, and other animals in places like Moraine Park or Horseshoe Park, so bring a set of binoculars.

Join free ranger-led activities including hikes and programs to learn more about the park's natural and human history. These educational presentations are fun as well as educational.

Photography: Use your camera to capture the beauty of the park. Without spending extra money, photography is a wonderful way to keep your memories alive.

Picnicking: In one of the approved picnic places in the park, enjoy a picnic with your own food. It's a reasonable and enjoyable way to have a meal while surrounded by beautiful scenery.

Camping and Dining Tips

Visiting a national park involves hefty costs, including food and camping. Here are some suggestions for reducing both costs:

Camping: A cheap option to enjoy the wilderness is to camp inside a park. The park has a number of campgrounds with different facilities and prices. To cut costs, think about camping at more affordable first-come, first-served campgrounds like Longs Peak or Timber Creek.

Backcountry Camping: Backcountry camping is an even more cost-effective choice. For a more private camping experience, get a backcountry camping permit from the park's visitor centers.

Cooking Your Meals: Use a grill or a camp stove to prepare your meals while you're camping. Cooking your own food allows you to eat outside and take in the scenery while saving money.

Bring Your Own Snacks and Water: To avoid paying exorbitant prices at gift shops or snack joints, bring your own snacks and reusable water bottles on trips and excursions.

Dining Outside the Park: If you'd rather eat outside the park, you might be able to locate more cheap options in neighboring cities like Estes Park or Grand Lake.

BYOB (Bring Your Own Bottle): To save buying bottled water, bring reusable water bottles that may be filled at the park's visitor centers or water fountains.

You can make the most of your trip to Rocky Mountain National Park without going overboard if you use these money-saving suggestions. Remember that a memorable and reasonably priced experience in this scenic wonderland may be created by thoughtful preparation, making use of park services, and appreciating the park's natural beauty.

Chapter 13. Conclusion

Fond Farewell to Rocky Mountain National Park

As your journey through Rocky Mountain National Park comes to an end, you'll probably feel overwhelmed and appreciative for the priceless encounters and spectacular scenery you've witnessed. Your heart and spirit have been permanently altered by the park's majestic peaks, verdant meadows, and diverse fauna. You won't forget the experiences of stargazing, viewing wildlife in its natural habitat, or wandering along picturesque paths for a very long time.

Think of the peace and calm you experienced in this natural refuge and the sensation of awe you felt when you were surrounded by such magnificent scenery. Keep in mind the friendships you formed with other tourists and the information you learned from ranger lectures and informative exhibits. And as you bid Rocky Mountain National Park a warm farewell, take into account the enduring influence it has had on your enjoyment of nature's beauty and the significance of protecting these priceless wilderness regions for future generations.

Your Next Adventure

One voyage comes to an end, another calls, and there are countless amazing places in the world just waiting to be discovered. Your trip to the Rocky Mountains probably whetted your appetite for additional exploration and travel. The options are endless, whether you decide to visit another national park, trek over a different mountain range, or immerse yourself in foreign cultures.

When choosing your next journey, take into account your passions and interests. Perhaps you'll visit more national parks to take in the varied beauties of nature or go to foreign locations to get a taste of other cultures. Accept the spirit of exploration that Rocky Mountain National Park has given you, and never forget that every journey offers fresh chances for development, learning, and amazement.

RMNP 2023

Always keep in mind the teachings from Rocky Mountain National Park as you travel the world: the value of conservation, how to treat animals with respect, and how to coexist with nature. Allow each place you visit to inspire you and enrich your life by traveling with an open mind and a curious heart.

In conclusion, Rocky Mountain National Park provides an experience that is both enthralling to the senses and nourishing to the soul. As you say goodbye to this magnificent wilderness, you'll take with you the tranquility of its serene beauty, the sounds of its wildlife, and the memory of its enormous sceneries. Your future travels should be filled with joy, curiosity, and a deep appreciation for the world's natural treasures. As you continue on your journey through life, let the lessons learned in this national park guide you in appreciating and protecting the wonders of nature. Travel safely!

Appendix

Useful Contacts and Emergency Information

It's crucial to be ready and know who to contact in case of emergencies or for general questions before starting any trip in Rocky Mountain National Park. Keep in mind the following helpful numbers and emergency information:

Park visitor Centers and Information:

The official website of Rocky Mountain National Park is a great source for the most recent information on park alerts, trail conditions, and other crucial updates. (Internet address: **www.nps.gov/romo**)

Throughout the park, there are a number of visitor centers where you may pick up maps, brochures, and more information from park rangers and personnel. These facilities are also excellent places to find out about educational and ranger programs.

Stations at Park Entrances:

Call **(970) 586-1206** to reach the East Entrance of the Beaver Meadows Visitor Center.

Phone: **(970) 586-1206** Fall River Visitor Center (West Entrance)

Call **(970) 627-3471** to reach the Kawuneeche Visitor Center at Grand Lake Entrance.

Services for Emergencies:

Emergency: Call **911** right away if there is a life-threatening situation.

Law Enforcement and Park Rangers:

Park Rangers: Park rangers can help, inform, and support you during your visit because they are quite knowledgeable about the park.

Call **(970) 586-1204** to report incidents or for help during the 24-hour emergency dispatch system.

Road Closures and Conditions:

Call **(970) 586-1222** for the most recent road conditions and any potential closures within the park.

Weather Prediction:

To make sure you're ready for any changes in the weather during your stay, check the National Weather Service for the most recent weather forecast for Rocky Mountain National Park.

Rescue and Search:

Call the park's emergency dispatch at **(970) 586-1204** in the event of a situation needing search and rescue. Keep in mind that search and rescue efforts may incur charges.

Make No Trace:

Rocky Mountain National Park adheres to the Leave No Trace philosophy, which places a strong emphasis on good outdoor behavior to reduce human effect on the ecosystem. Learn about these guidelines and put them into action while you are there.

Medical Facilities Nearby:

Call **(970) 586-2317** to reach Estes Park Medical Center in Estes Park, Colorado.

Call **(970) 887-5800** to reach Middle Park Medical Center in Granby, Colorado.

Cellular and Wi-Fi Coverage:

In some parts of the park, there might not be adequate cell phone coverage. Within the park's boundaries, there is no public Wi-Fi.

You can guarantee a risk-free and delightful trip to Rocky Mountain National Park by keeping these vital contacts and emergency information close at hand. While exploring this breathtaking area, never compromise on safety and always be prepared for changing weather conditions.

Printed in Great Britain
by Amazon

31629408R00056